DMC ANTIQUE COLLECTION

東欧刺繍のモチーフ＆パターン

クロスステッチ フォークロア

Cross-Stitch Folklore

Contents

ウクライナ　6　UKRAINE
女神の刺繍　Goddesses in embroidery

ルーマニア　10　ROMANIA
お国柄と模様　Nationalities and patterns

ブルガリア　16　BULGARIA
赤・黒・白　Red, black and white

ハンガリー　22　HUNGARY
日常着の刺繍　Embroidery for daily clothes

マケドニア & クロアチア　26　MACEDONIA & CROATIA
刺繍の役割　Role of embroidery

コーカサス　28　CAUCASUS
"生命の樹"　"The tree of life"

チェコ & スロバキア　30　CZECH & SLOVAKIA
花嫁からの贈り物　Gifts from a bride

トルコ　34　TURKEY
タオルに縁飾り　Decorated towels

ポーランド　38　POLAND
魔よけの刺繍　Embroidery as a charm

セルビア & モンテネグロ　40　SERBIA & MONTENEGRO
美しいクロスステッチ　Beautiful cross-stitch

その他　46　OTHERS

ステッチ & パターン　49　STITCHES & PATTERNS

Written by Makiko Komiya　小宮真喜子

This book introduces the embroideries of Turkey, Macedonia and Caucasus other than of Eastern Europe.

ブラウスでもスカートでも、帽子やスカーフでも、なんでもいいのです。あなたの旅が刺繍探しのためのものなら、ぜひ東欧においでください。かの地では午後の陽だまりのそこかしこで、素朴な生地に細密な刺繍を施す女性たちの姿があります。赤や青のほぐした糸を、おばあさんの使っている針に通す、小学生ぐらいのポーランドの女の子がいます。民族衣装ほど正装ではないものの、フォークロア調の白いブラウスに連続した模様の胸飾りを刺す、ルーマニアのお嬢さんがいます。エルベ川の東から黒海にいたる、東欧諸国に流れる緩やかな時は今なお、女性たちの生活に愛と潤いをもたらす刺繍文化を育み続けています。

かの地の刺繍の独自性に早くから着目したのは、DMC と刺繍家のテレーズ・ド・ディルモン女史でした。1746 年、フランス初の染色工場をはじめたジャン・アンリ・ドルフュス氏の後継者で、そのころ当主だったジャン・ドルフュス・ミエッグとの強い信頼関係からディルモン女史はミュルーズ近郊に移住を決意します。DMC の協賛を得て、ミュルーズに刺繍学校を設立。それだけでなく、それまで人々に長く受け継がれていた刺繍の技法を集大成し、なんと『手芸百科事典』を出版します。世界中の女性に刺繍の魅力を広めた女史こそ、刺繍の第一人者に違いありません。ちなみに DMC の名称は、ドルフュスの D とミエッグの M にカンパニーの C からできています。

パリから東に 465 キロ。花とコロンバージュと呼ばれる、漆喰と梁の木組みの家々が並ぶミュルーズの町はかつて、フランスの産業革命発祥の地でした。そして渦中どころか、なんとDMC の工場で産業革命の火ぶたが切られたのです。

澄んだ空気と青い空にコウノトリが舞うアルザス地方のミュルーズの町に、あなたもぜひおいでください。本書を通じて、素晴らしい刺繍の世界をご堪能いただけたら幸いです。

文 吉村葉子

本書掲載図案の出典：ミュルーズ DMC

If you set out on a journey to look for embroidery, whether on blouses, skirts, hats or scarfs, you should visit Eastern Europe. You can find women here and there in the afternoon sun, embroidering fine patterns on simple fabrics, a young Polish girl of elementary school age passing red or blue braided threads through her grandmother's needle or a young Romanian woman embroidering running patterns on the front of her white blouse in a folkloric design, which is not as formal as folk costumes.

The gentle flow of time in Eastern European countries lying from the east of the Elbe River to the Black Sea, continues to nurture the culture of embroidery that enriches the lives of women. It was DMC and an embroiderer, Thérèse de Dillmont, who focused on the uniqueness of Eastern European embroidery. She decided to move to the suburbs of Mulhouse for the trusted relationship between her and Jean Dollfus-Mieg, the family head at that time and also a successor of Jean-Henri Dollfus who had founded the first dyeing factory in France in 1746. Under the support of DMC, she established an embroidery school. Furthermore, she published "Encyclopèdie des Ouvrerages de Dames", a compilation of embroidery techniques which had been handed down by many people for a long time. She, who introduced the pleasure of embroidery to women all around the world, was undoubtedly a leading person in the world of embroidery.

The name of DMC consists of D for Dollfus, M for Mieg and C for Company. Located 465 km east of Paris. Mulhouse which is lined with flowers and the half-timbered houses, called "Colombages", was the birthplace of the industrial revolution in France. DMC factory was exactly the place where the revolution began. Why not visit Mulhouse with clean air and blue skies with wheeling storks. It would give us a great pleasure if you could enjoy the wonderful world of embroidery through this book.

Written by Yoko Yoshimura

Source of the patterns published in this book : DMC, Mulhouse

UKRAINE ウクライナ

女神の刺繍

刺繍の模様では、人々の生活に身近な動植物や信仰、自身の願望などが具象的、抽象的に表される。花は多く取り入れられているモチーフで、バラやチューリップ、カーネーションなど多様な花がデザイン化されて衣装を飾った。これらの花はギリシア神話に見られるような女神をイメージして用いられたと思われる。中でも美や愛を象徴するバラは、日本人が桜を愛でるようにヨーロッパでは広く好まれている。ウクライナでもバラの刺繍は多く用いられ、東ウクライナでは具象的なデザイン、西ウクライナでは幾何学的なデザインが見られる。

Goddesses in embroidery

Embroidery patterns show familiar animals and plants, beliefs and wishes in representational or abstract designs. Flower motifs were often used in embroidery. A variety of flowers such as roses, tulips and carnations were designed for embroidery to embellish costumes. The flower motifs seem to symbolize the goddesses in Greek mythology. Particularly, the rose, a symbol of beauty and love, was popular among European people just like the cherry blossom is loved by the Japanese. Also in Ukraine, rose motifs are often used in embroidery. Representational designs appear in Eastern Ukraine and geometrical designs in Western Ukraine.

Wrap : Design by Naoko Shimoda (Reference Work)

UKRAINE

8

> page 54-55

ROMANIA ルーマニア

10

> page 56-57

お国柄と模様

東欧の民族衣装にほどこされる刺繍は、各地域ごとに特徴のある独自のデザインが用いられている。これらの国々の刺繍は、他国との支配や侵略を繰り返していた歴史により、関係した国の文化や宗教などの影響が見られるものも少なくない。ルーマニアはトルコやロシアの支配を受けた歴史をもち、ハンガリー系やドイツ系をはじめとする異民族が住む国のため、同じ国の中でも地域により、衣装の着方や刺繍の模様にそれぞれの民族の独自性が表れている。トルコの支配を受けたハンガリーやブルガリアでもまた、隣接する国々の民族の文化が入り混じり、様々な模様が見られる。

Nationalities and patterns

The patterns of embroidery embellishing the folk costumes found in Eastern Europe have different regional characteristics. Many of the patterns have been influenced by the cultures or religions of foreign countries which invaded or ruled Eastern European countries. In Romania, which experienced the rules of Turkey and Russia and has several ethnic groups including Hungarian and German Romanians, the peculiarities of ethnic groups in different regions are shown in the style of dressing or embroidery patterns. Also in Hungary and Bulgaria, which experienced the rule of Turkey, embroidery patterns reflect different cultures including those from neighboring countries.

II

> page 57

> page 60

ROMANIA

13

Easy Pants (Reference Work)

ROMANIA

> page 58-59

15

> page 61

BULGARIA ブルガリア

Small Bag > page 67

赤・黒・白

東欧の刺繍には赤と黒の糸が多く使用される。ブルガリアの刺繍では赤、黒、白が基本の3色であり、それぞれに意味を持つ。民間信仰によると赤は太陽と繁殖力のある男性の象徴や魔除け、黒は地球の色で先祖の守護を象徴するとされ、白は光、水、豊穣を表す。これらの色の意味するところはキリスト教やイスラム教の教えが関係していると考えられる。キリスト教で赤は温かい血、すなわち愛の象徴とされ、白は清楚、神秘、神聖をイメージする聖なる色とされている。また黒は悪や死を意味することが多いが、キリスト教やイスラム教の世界では禁欲の色としている。

Red, black and white

In Eastern Europe, red and black threads are often used for embroidery. In Bulgaria, red, black and white are the three basic colors used in embroidery and have their own meanings. According to folk beliefs, red symbolizes the sun and virility and serves as a charm against evils, white symbolizes light, water and fertility, and black, the color representing the earth, symbolizes ancestral guardianship. These meanings are considered to be related to the Christian and Islamic faiths. For Christianity, red symbolizes warm blood, i.e., love, and white, which is regarded as a sacred color, symbolizes cleanliness, mysteriousness and sacredness. Black, which generally means evil and death, is considered to be the color of abstinence for both the Christian and Islamic religions.

> page 62,70

17

> page 63

> page 64-65

BULGARIA

> page 65, 68

BULGARIA

20

> page 70

> page 66

HUNGARY ハンガリー

Muffler > page 73

日常着の刺繡

民族衣装を大切にする東欧の国でも、日常には一般的な「洋服」が多く着られている。それでも地方の村々を訪れると、日常の中に伝統的な装いを見ることができる。女性はブラウスとスカートまたは丈の長いシュミーズドレスにエプロンと帯、ベストを組み合わせ、男性はシャツにズボン、帯、ベストがその伝統的な組み合わせである。どの国でも第2次世界大戦前には、手の込んだ刺繡をほどこした民族衣装を日常でも身につけていたようであるが、戦後の近代化の発展で日常着としての着用は減り、刺繡においても晴れ着以外に華やかなものは少なくなった。

Embroidery for daily clothes

Nowadays, ordinary clothes are worn in everyday life even in the countries which value folk costumes. However, we can see traditional fashions when visiting villages in the countryside. Women wear a blouse and a skirt or a long dress with an apron, a sash and a vest. Men wear a shirt and trousers with a sash and a vest. Before World War II, people in Eastern Europe used to wear folk costumes with elaborate embroidery. In keeping with the modernization after the war, they came to wear the costumes less and less in everyday life, and gorgeous embroidery can rarely be seen except in holiday clothes.

> page 71

HUNGARY

Bag : Design by Naoko Shimoda (Reference Work)

MACEDONIA & CROATIA
マケドニア & クロアチア

刺繡の役割

国が隣接し、多民族が暮す東欧のような地域では、民族衣装は自己を示すための名刺代わりともいえる。服の構成、着こなし、色合い、装飾などで、それを着用する人の民族の属性、国籍、出身地、年齢や社会的地位、さらにはその服の用途がわかる。その中に表されたさまざまな模様は、一人一人を見分ける手段のひとつとして大切な役割を持つ。そしてその表現方法として、刺繡という身近な装飾技法が用いられた。糸と針があれば模様を自在にデザインすることができる刺繡の表現方法は、長い年月の中で昇華され、美しい伝統模様をつくりだした。

Role of embroidery

In Eastern Europe where each country neighbors on foreign countries and several ethnic groups coexist in a single country, ethnic costumes function as a kind of identification card. The outfit, the style of dressing, the color coordination and the decorations seen in costumes represent nationality, ethnic characteristics, age, social status and the use for costumes. Embroidery, a simple technique for freely embellishing costumes only with thread and needle, was introduced as a way to draw patterns which play an important role in identification. Over a long period of time their embroidery was refined to create beautiful traditional patterns.

> page 74-75

CAUCASUS コーカサス

28

"生命の樹"

刺繍の模様は単に服を美しく飾り立てるだけではなく、日々の生活の中での様々な願いを込めて繡い表されている。コーカサス地方の刺繍模様に見られるような"生命の樹"と呼ばれる立木模様は、豊穣や生命を象徴する聖樹として、ヨーロッパからアジアにいたるまでの広い地域で見られる。孔雀の模様は不滅や復活の象徴にされる。ほかにも十字架、太陽、鳩、葡萄など、それぞれの地域の信仰に由来する自然や動植物などの模様が刺繍に取り入れられた。

"The tree of life"

Patterns of embroidery not only decorate clothes, but also represent several wishes that people make in everyday life. The pattern of a standing tree shown in embroidered works from Caucasus, which is called "the tree of life", the sacred tree symbolizing fertility and life, is used in embroidery in a wide area ranging from Europe to Asia. The peacock symbolizes immortality and resurrection. The patterns of religious symbol, nature, animals and plants such as the cross, the sun, pigeons and grapes were derived from the beliefs of each region.

> page 76-77

CZECH & SLOVAKIA
チェコ & スロバキア

花嫁からの贈り物

豊かに刺繍された民族衣装は主に、婚礼をはじめとした人生の節目ふしめの儀式や新年、クリスマス、毎日曜のミサに見られるような祭礼用の晴れ着として着られる。これらの衣装の刺繍は女性によって自分のため、家族や愛する人のために一針一針に愛情を込めて繍われた。チェコやブルガリアでは、母は娘に糸紡ぎ、織り、刺繍といったあらゆる手仕事を伝え、娘は結婚や成人の儀式に自ら刺繍をほどこした服を身につけた。男女の出会いの場となる集まりでは、娘は競って刺繍や織りの技を披露し、自らをアピールしたようである。結婚式では、この日のために用意した豪華に刺繍された衣装が着られ、花婿には身につける刺繍の品物が花嫁から贈られた。

Gifts from a bride

Folk costumes with colorful embroidery are usually worn as holiday clothes for festivals or festivities including a variety of rites, such as weddings, New Year's celebration, Christmas and mass on Sundays. Women embroidered holiday costumes for those they love and for themselves. In Czech Republic and Bulgaria, all handiwork skills including spinning, weaving and embroidery used to be handed down from mother to daughter. Young women embroidered their own clothes and wore them at their coming of age ceremony or wedding. At parties which may provide them with opportunities to meet young men, they used to compete to show their handicraft skills. At weddings, people were decked out in gorgeously embroidered clothes that were made only for these occasions, and the bride gave the bridegroom embroidered articles to wear.

> page 80

Muffler & Skirt : Design by nooy > page 80

CZECH & SLOVAKIA

TURKEY トルコ

タオルに縁飾り

刺繍は服ばかりでなく、枕カバー、クッションカバー、ハンカチーフ、壁の装飾用の布など、東欧の各地域で共通して用いられてきた様々な生活用品にもほどこされる。その中でも念入りに刺繍された品々は、各地で嫁入り道具のひとつとしても扱われた歴史をもつ。トルコではタオルにほどこされる刺繍が多く見られ、"生命の樹"、花、建物を表したボーダー柄の刺繍がタオルの両端を飾る。そのタオルは地域によって様々な用途があり、腰帯として、来客者を迎えるための大きなパンをのせる布として、また教会の飾りなどの儀式用としても用いられた。

Decorated towels

Embroidery decorates not only clothes but also articles for daily use, including pillowcases, cushion cases, handkerchiefs and cloth for wall decoration, which have been used in common throughout Eastern Europe. Among them, the elaborately embroidered articles are regarded as bridal trousseau in various regions. Embroidered towels are common in Turkey. Patterns representing the tree of life, flowers and buildings are placed at both ends of towels. In accordance with local customs, towels can be used for different purposes, such as belts or sashes, or as mats on which a large loaf of bread for guests is placed or as decorations for religious services.

> page 81

35

> page 82

TURKEY

36

Hat : Design by Asae Misono > page 84

37

> page 83

POLAND ポーランド

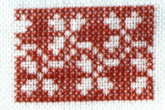

魔よけの刺繍

東欧の刺繍でどの国にも共通するのが細かな連続模様のボーダー柄であろう。ポーランドの刺繍に見られるような、幾何学模様の花をデザインした連続模様が服を飾る。これらのボーダー柄は主に男性のシャツや女性のシュミーズの襟元、袖口、裾まわりに見ることができる。シャツやシュミーズは、もとは白地の亜麻製の肌着だった。この縁に、装飾を加えたのである。これら縁飾りの刺繍は簡素な服に彩りを与えただけでなく、袖口などから悪霊が身体に入り込まないよう、また模様に込められた願いがこれらの口から外に抜け出ていかないようにという呪術的意味を込めて繍われている。

Embroidery as a charm

An embroidery design common in Eastern Europe is a series of small patterns. As shown in Polish embroidery works, a series of geometric patterns or flower motifs decorate costumes. Such decorations are mostly found on neckline, cuffs and hems of men's shirts or women's chemises which used to be white linen underwear. Such embroidery not only decorates simple clothes but also functions as a charm for keeping evil spirits from entering the body or keeping wishes put into patterns from going out through cuffs.

> page 85

> page 85-86

SERBIA & MONTENEGRO セルビア&モンテネグロ

美しいクロスステッチ

クロスステッチは平織地のひと目ひと目にクロスをつくりながら模様を表す手法である。この規則的な手法は連続模様や左右対称の模様などの刺繍に適し、それほど高度な技術を持たない人でも容易に刺繍ができる。今はクロスステッチ専用のキャンバス地が存在するが、民族衣装に見られるようなかつてのクロスステッチは、女性たちが麻や綿を紡いで織った平織地にほどこされていた。手織りでしっかりと織られた生地のひと目ずつを針ですくい、刺し進むクロスステッチは、クロスがとても細かく目が詰んでおり、美しく繊細な模様を表している。

Beautiful cross-stitch

Cross-stitch is a technique of embroidery stitching a cross on each thread of plain cloth. This orderly technique is suitable for stitching a series of patterns or symmetrical patterns, enabling beginners to stitch easily. In the past, unlike in the present day in which we have a special canvas for cross-stitch, women used to cross-stitch on plain cloth woven from linen or cotton for folk costumes. Fine cross-stitch using a technique of picking up each thread of tightly woven cloth form exquisite patterns.

> page 88

SERBIA & MONTENEGRO

> page 90-91

43

44

SERBIA & MONTENEGRO

Cotton Dress : Design by Yoko Nogi > page 92-94

OTHERS

46

Japanese Kimono : Design by Mayumi Katsuya

> page 80

東欧を中心としたクロスステッチの刺繍は、女性のたしなみとして母から娘へ受け継がれていたものが多い。日々の生活の中で育まれてきた刺繍は、素朴ながらも芸術に値するほどの美しさを備えている。ひたすら刺繍をすることは忙しい現代にはそぐわない時間の流れではあるが、ゆったりとした時代に時間を戻し、ひと針に願いを込めて繍い進めるひと時を過ごすことも大切にしたいものである。

Cross-stitch, a craft culture, common in Eastern Europe, have usually been handed down from mother to daughter as an essential achievement of women. The works done by ordinary people in everyday life are as beautiful as works of art in spite of their simplicity. Although nothing but embroidering does not seem to fit in with busy modern life, we should value the way of spending time stitching while making wishes at a leisurely pace in good old days.

STITCHES & PATTERNS

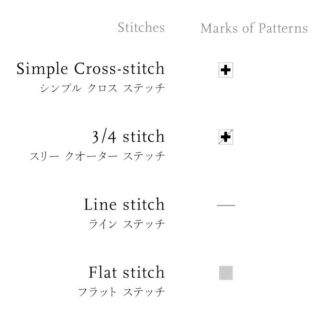

★本書ではおもにDMCリネン28カウント（110目）にDMC25番糸でステッチしています。
★糸の色はカラーナンバーで表示しています。

DMC LINEN (count 28) and DMC Mouliné Spécial® are mainly used in this book.
Thread colors are indicated by the numbers.

STITCHES

刺し方手順の奇数番号は針を裏から表に出し、偶数番号は針を表から裏に入れます。
Pass needle from wrong side to right side for odd-numbered steps and do the opposite for even-numbered steps.

Simple Cross-stitch
シンプル クロス ステッチ

(A)と(B)とふた通りの刺しすすめ方があります。
どちらで刺す場合も上に重なる糸の向きがつねに同じになるように刺すことがポイントです。
糸がつれないように、2目以上あくときは一度糸を切ってから刺しはじめるときれいです。

There are two ways to work, (A) and (B).
In both ways, make sure all the top threads of the crosses lie in the same direction.
When leaving a space of 2 or more stitches, cut off thread and start again.

A. 往復の針運びで仕上げていく方法　Line of Cross-stitches in two journeys

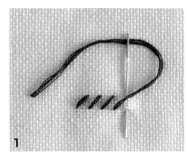 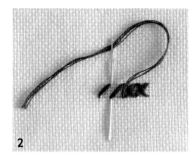 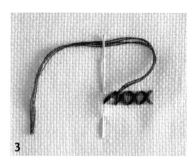

左下から右上に刺していき(1)、クロスをつくりながら戻っていきます(2)。1列を刺し終えたら下にすすみ、つぎの列を同様に刺します(3)。
Bring needle up at bottom left and down at top right (1), stitch back making crosses (2) and begin next row in the same way (3).

B. クロスをひとつずつ仕上げながら刺す方法　Line of Cross-stitches worked one by one

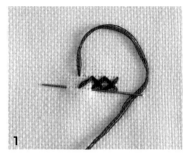 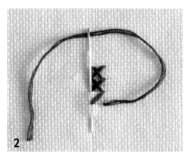 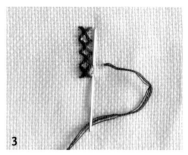

クロスする下側の糸は左下から右上に刺し、上側の糸は左上から右下に刺し、右から左に刺しすすめます(1)。
下にすすむときは(2)の針運びで刺し、次列を続けて刺すときは(3)の針運びで上に刺しすすめます。列ごとに下上交互に刺しましょう。
Bring needle up at bottom left, down at top right, up at top left and down at bottom right and repeat leftward (1), work a stitch as indicated by (2) to move downward and begin next row as indicated by (3). Work rows alternately up and down.

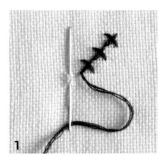 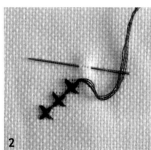

斜めに刺していくときも同じ要領。
(1)の針運びで斜め下に刺しすすめ、
次列を刺すときは(2)の針運びで斜め上に刺しあげていきます。

Begin in the same way as the above and work diagonally left downward as indicated by (1) and work next row diagonally right upward as indicated by (2).

3/4 stitch
スリー クオーター ステッチ

斜線をなめらかに表現するのに適したステッチ。
使われる場所によってステッチの向きが変わり、aの向きに刺せば右上がなめらかなラインに、
bの向きに刺せば左上がなめらかなラインになるという具合です。
ひとマスに色違いの2色を向き合わせに刺すこともでき、
このようにするとすき間のないなめらかな色替えができます。

This stitch is suitable for drawing slanted lines and may slant in any direction as shown on a and b according to designs.
Two stitches in two colors may be worked face to face in a square for smooth color change of slanted lines.

a
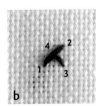
b
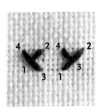

Holbein stitch
ホルベイン ステッチ

画家の名前で親しまれているステッチ。
ぜんぶが同じ長さの針目からできていて、往復の針運びでひとつのラインに仕上げていきます。
左から右に刺しますが、右から左に刺すこともできます。

This stitch is well known for the name of the painter.
Each line is worked in two journeys.
Work a line of running stitches from left to right or right to left.

Straight line 直線のライン　　Diagonal line 斜めのライン　　Stair line 階段のライン　　Square line 四角のライン

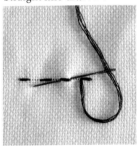 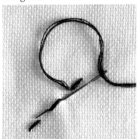  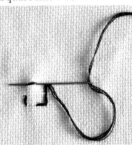

布目を同じ目数だけすくっていき、ラインの最後まで刺したら方向を変え、はじめに残した部分を刺しながら戻ります。
階段のラインをつくるときは水平のステッチを刺し、垂直のステッチで刺し戻りながら階段状に完成させます。
四角のラインは四角を囲むように刺し、戻りながら残した目を刺して完成させます。

Work a line of stitches leaving spaces equal in length and stitch back along the line filling the spaces.
Stairs may be formed with upward horizontal stitches and downward vertical stitches.
Squares may be formed with stitches framing a square and return stitches filling the spaces.

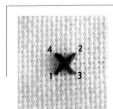

とび柄を刺すときは、
ぜんぶの模様を刺し終えたあとに
ひとつずつ刺し、
糸始末もひとつずつしましょう。
Isolated motifs should be stitched individually after working all patterns.

★本書では表記上、
ラインステッチと重なるときのスリークオーターステッチは、
斜線の向きを逆向きに表示しています。
ステッチにはストレートステッチ、ランニングステッチ、
サテンステッチも使用。
図案は原典に準拠して表記しています。

Diagonal lines of 3/4 stitches show the direction of stitches but the opposite lines used with line stitches.
Straight st., Running st. and Satin st. also used.
The marks in the charts are based on the originals.

Plaited Slav stitch
プレーテッド スラブ ステッチ

"スラブ風三つ編み" "ハンガリアン三つ編み刺し" ともよばれている伝統的な手法で、長短の斜めのステッチを交差させていきます。
チェコの赤いボーダー(p.32)の地埋め(フラット ステッチ)に用いています。

This stitch is a traditional technique, also called as Slavic or Hungarian plaited stitch.
Diagonal long and short stitches are crossed each other to form a plait.
Used in Czech red border (p.32).

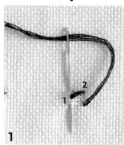
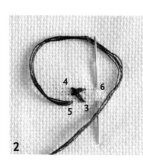
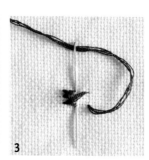
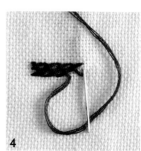

はじめに1から2の短いステッチを刺します(1)。3-6をくり返して右に刺しすすめ(2,3)、列の最後にも短いステッチを刺します(4)。
最初と最後の短いステッチは補助ステッチで、列の端をきっちり埋めるために刺しています。

Begin with a short stitch from 1 to 2 (1), repeat 3 to 6 rightward (2,3) and end with a short stitch (4).
The first and last stitches are auxiliary stitches for filling the both border ends.

Kelim stitch
ケリム ステッチ

じゅうたんの織り方を模したとされる伝統的な手法ですが、
刺し方はかんたん、ステッチの向きを決め、あとは一列ずつ向きを変えて刺していくだけです。
チェコのボーダー(p.32)の黄色の地埋めに横向きに刺して用いています。

This stitch is a traditional and simple technique imitating carpet weaving.
Work first row in a single direction and change direction alternately for each row.
Used in Czech yellow border (p.32).

1,2の針運びではじめのステッチを刺し、次からは同じ方向に刺すことをくり返します。
2列めは向きを変えて刺し、これをくり返してV字模様をつくっていきます。

Work a first stitch from 1 to 2 and repeat in the same direction.
Begin next row in the opposite direction and repeat to form V-shaped patterns.

Cross-stitch Variation
クロス ステッチ ヴァリエーション

縦長のクロスステッチを一列ごとに半目ずつずらして刺します。
チェコのボーダー(p.32)のオレンジの地埋めに用いています。

Work a row of oblong cross-stitches downward and begin next row with a half stitch so as to deviate the row from the first row by a half stitch. Used in Czech orange border (p.32).

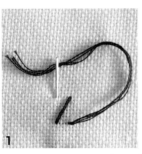
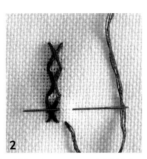
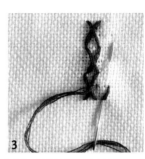
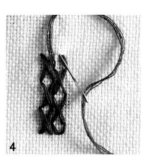

1列めは2倍の長さのクロスステッチを下方向に刺し(1)、2列めは半目分をV字形に刺してから、上に刺しすすめ(2,3)、列の最後は半目分を逆V字形に刺します(4)。これをくり返して模様をつくっていきます。

Work a row of cross-stitches double in length downward (1), begin next row with a half stitch in V shape and work the row upward with cross-stitches (2,3), and work a half stitch in inverted V shape at the end (4). Repeat 1 to 4.

Line stitch Variation
ライン ステッチ ヴァリエーション

上下で返し縫いをくり返しながら直線をつくっていくステッチ。
チェコの赤いボーダー(p.32)の白いラインは、このステッチで刺しています。

Repeat back stitches alternately above and below the previous stitch to make a line. Used in white lines in Czech red border (p.32).

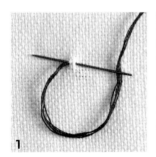
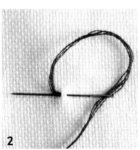
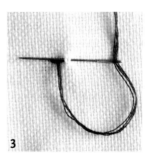
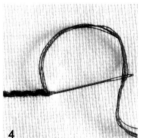

左から右に1目刺し、上に半目戻って(1)から1目刺し、下に半目戻ってから1目刺します(2,3)。
上下交互に半目ずつ戻りながら右にすすめます(4)。

Work a half stitch from left to right(1), stitch halfway back above the previous stitch and work a stitch (2), stitch halfway back below the previous stitch and work a stitch (3), repeat as required (4).

UKRAINE page 6, 8-9

color numbers

✚ 3799

▲ 349

ROMANIA page 10-11

color numbers

◆ 3345 ✚ 310
◉ 334   △ 309
▣ 3750 ▲ 349
■ 823   ✶ 444

ROMANIA   page 14

color numbers

▣	794	▲	350
◻	791	▽	402
■	939	★	3832
✚	3799	✖	725
△	304		

ROMANIA page 12-13, 15

color numbers

◯ 973 ☐ 340 Ⅱ 729

◇ 500 ▣ 809

◈ 3346 ■ 823

◆ 3815 ✚ 3799

◆ 501 △ 326

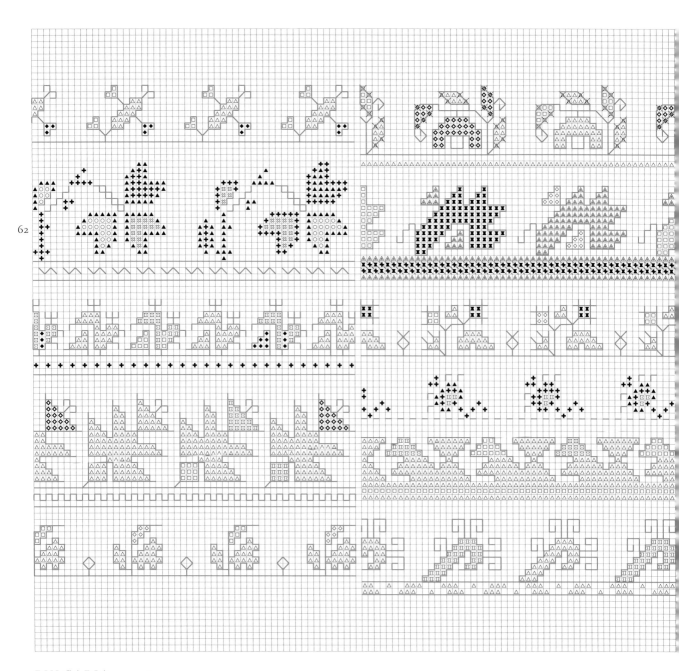

BULGARIA page 16-17

color numbers

○	832	◆	319	△	900	⊠	726
◇	500	□	931	▲	349	Ⅱ	727
◈	503	▣	794	◬	351	▮	742
◉	3815	✜	3799	▲	321	⊠	554
◆	905	✚	310	▼	3776		

BULGARIA page 18-19

BULGARIA page 16, 21

color numbers

⊙	610	▲	349	Ⅱ	727
◈	907	▽	3856	■	444
◆	905	▽	900		
▪	334	★	601		
▪	823	Ⅱ	725		

BULGARIA page 19

color numbers

✚ 310	𝕀 726
■ 312	◈ 3347
△ 347	▼ 3776

SERBIA & MONTENEGRO   page 41

color numbers

☆ 3326   ★ 600
✠ 932   ◎ 3362
✚ 3799   ⚠ 3740

BULGARIA page 16, 20

color numbers

- ◆ 500
- ▥ 809
- ■ 311
- ✚ 3799
- ▲ 349
- ⊠ 725

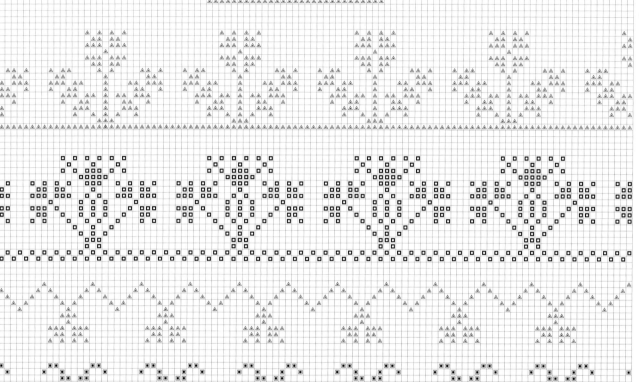

HUNGARY page 23

color numbers

▪ 312

☐ 931

▲ 347

HUNGARY page 22

73

color numbers

- ● 938
- ⊕ B5200
- ▫ 995
- △ 666
- ■ 336
- ▲ 335

74

MACEDONIA & CROATIA
page 26-27

color numbers

◉	632	◆	3345
◘	920	◻	3760
●	3371	◼	3746
◈	3053	△	817
◇	702	✕	3821

CAUCASUS page 28-29

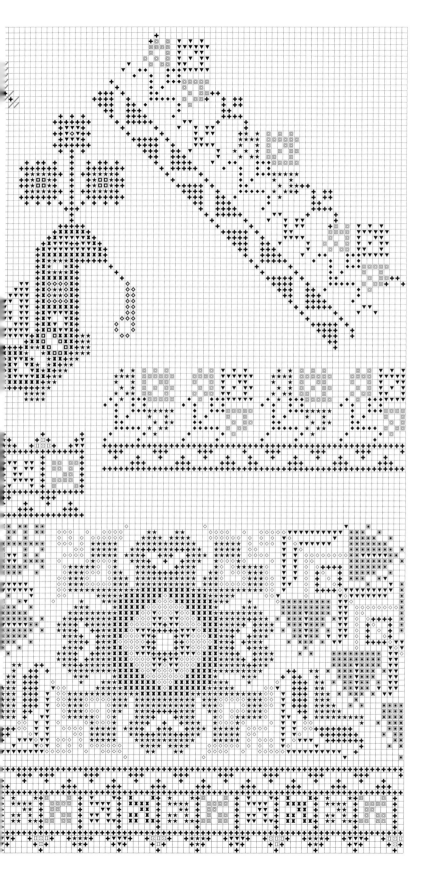

color numbers

◉ 371	◘ 3839	▨ 743
◇ 597	✚ 844	◆ 611
◈ 3363	▼ 722	
▣ 3840	★ 3832	
▪ 792	⊠ 745	

CZECH & SLOVAKIA page 32-33

CZECH & SLOVAKIA page 30-31, 48

color numbers

◯ 543	◉ 341
◎ 839	✚ 317
◼ 610	+ 413
◆ 524	✚ 3799

TURKEY page 34

color numbers

● 814	◆ 895	▲ 347
◈ 3768	■ 930	▼ 920
◉ 501	✜ 926	☆ 352
◇ 924	✚ 3799	✖ 726

TURKEY page 35, 37

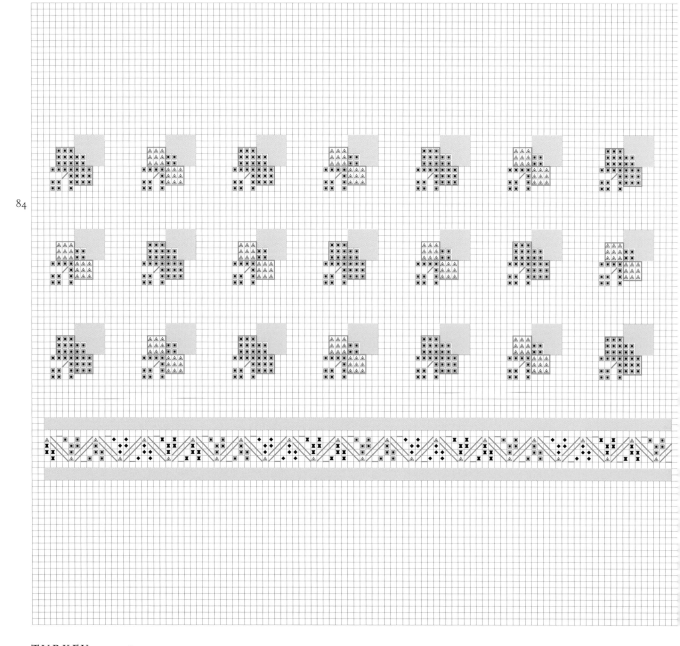

TURKEY page 36

color numbers

◆ 3364   △ 350
■ 932   ✗ 743

POLAND page 38-39

color numbers

✚ 310   ▲ 321
△ 817   ★ 309

POLAND page 39

color numbers

✚ 310

△ 817

★ 309

OTHERS page 46-47

color numbers

◇ 3848

✚ 3799

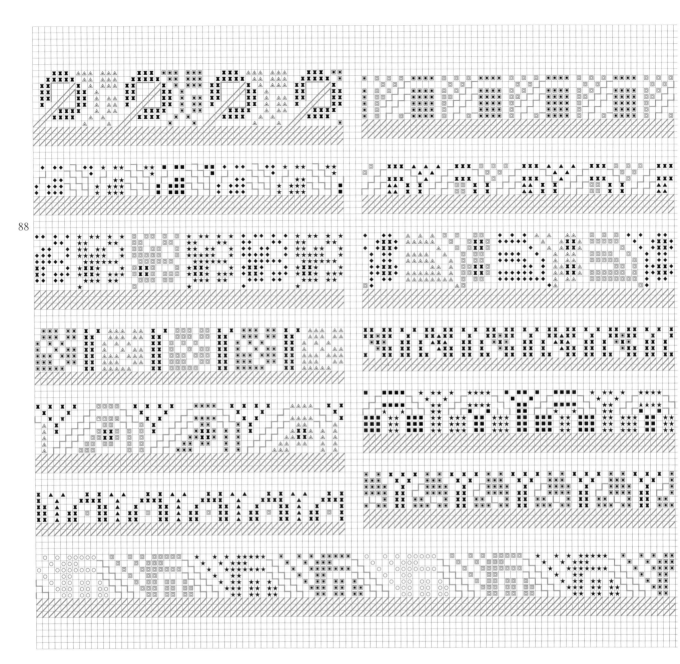

SERBIA & MONTENEGRO page 40, 43

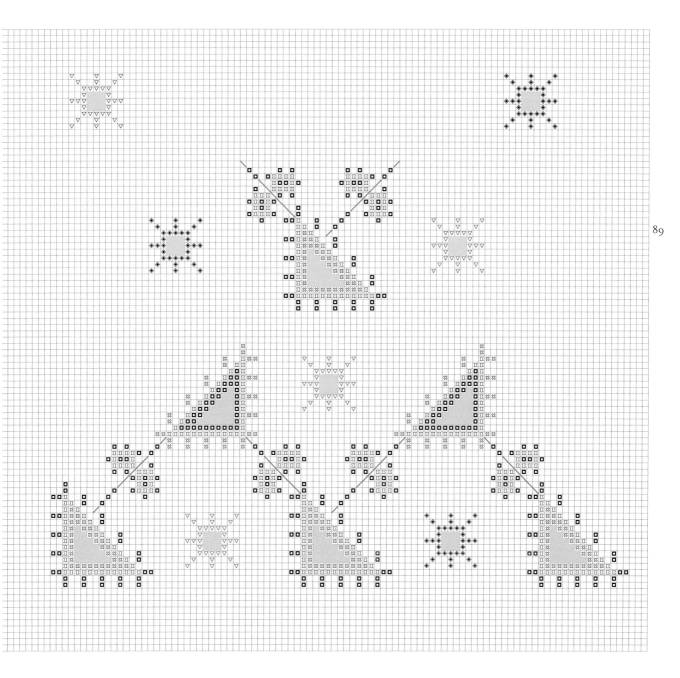

SERBIA & MONTENEGRO page 42

color numbers

✚ 310		■ 930		✸ 831	
□ 931		▣ 3750		▪ 932	
◉ 3772		▲ 815		◊ 3363	
▵ 777		✾ 522			

SERBIA & MONTENEGRO
page 44-45

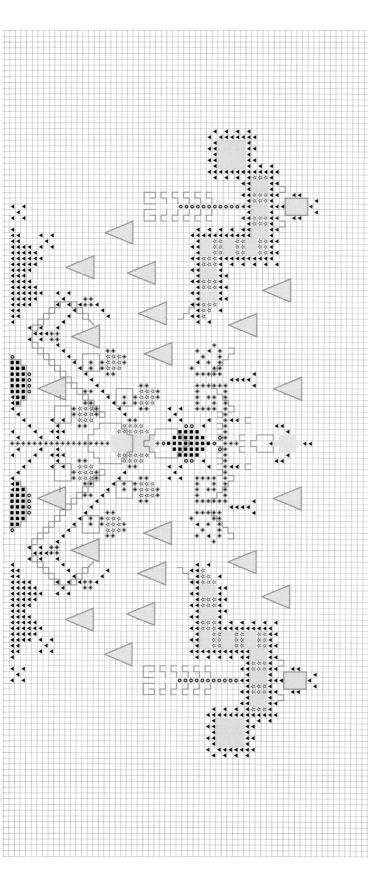

color numbers

- ◉ 838
- ◈ 500
- ■ 792
- ▲ 817
- ☆ 3326

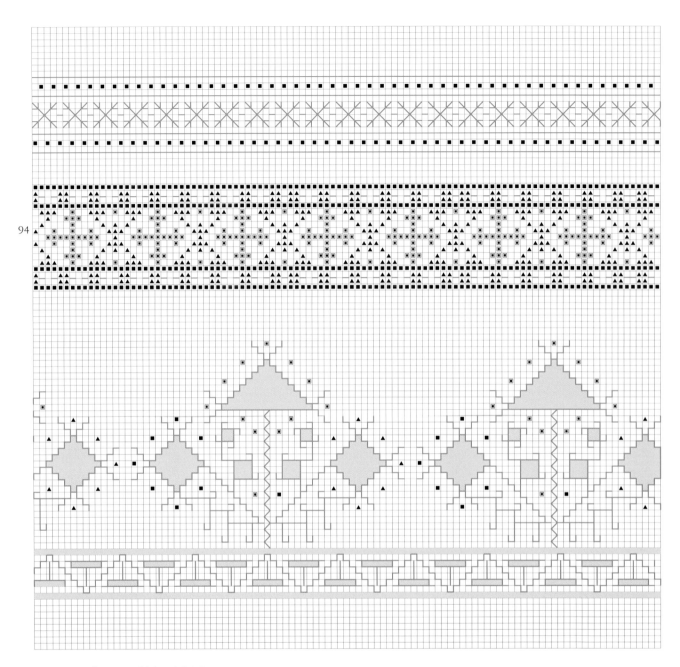

SERBIA & MONTENEGRO page 44-45

color numbers

▫ 792
▪ 939
▲ 817

Creators of Works

Naoko Shimoda
Handicraft artist. She organizes the handicraft school "MOTIF".
"Shimoda Naoko no Syugeijyutsu" (CHIKUMASHOBO).
p.7, p.24-25.

下田直子
手芸作家。手芸スクール「オフィスMOTIF」主宰。
著書に『下田直子の手芸術』(筑摩書房)他。
p7, p.24-25の作品をデザイン&制作。

Mayumi Katsuya
Designer. She established "how to live".
"Tsukuroi Note" (BUNKA PUBLISHING BUREAU).
p.47.

勝屋まゆみ
デザイナー。布雑貨のブランド how to live 主宰。
著書に『繕いノート』(文化出版局)他。
p.47の作品をデザイン&制作。

Natsuko Wakayama／Yoshika Hirayama
Fashion designers. They established "nooy".
p.30 (muffler), p.31. www.nooy.jp

若山夏子／平山良佳
ファッションデザイナー。ブランド nooy 主宰。
p.30(マフラー), p.31の作品をデザイン&制作。

Asae Misono
Freelance designer.
"Graphic Knit" (MAGAZINELAND).
p.36.

三園麻絵
フリーランスデザイナー。
著書に『グラフィックニット』(マガジンランド)他。
p.36の作品をデザイン&制作。

Yoko Nogi
Sewing designer.
"KIDS WARDROBE" (NIHON VOGUE SHA).
p.44-45.

野木陽子
ソーイング作家。大人服&子供服を中心に作品を発表。
著書に『着ごこちのいい小さな子の服』(日本ヴォーグ社)他。
p.44-45の作品をデザイン&制作。

Ayako Otsuka
Embroiderer. She established "Embroidery Studio Ecru".
"WHITE WORK EMBROIDERY" (NIHON VOGUE SHA).
p.14, p.28-29.

大塚あや子
刺繍作家。Embroidery Studio Ecru 主宰。
著書に『白い糸の刺繍』(日本ヴォーグ社)他。
p.14, p.28-29の作品を刺繍。

Hisako Nishisu
Embroiderer. Director of Japan Art Craft Association.
"DRAWN THREAD EMBROIDERY"(BUNKA PUBLISHING BUREAU).
p.6, p.8-9, p.18, p.19, p.22(muffler), p.23, p.30, p.31, p.32,
p.33, p.35, p.38, p.39, p.41, p43, p47, p.48 .
Techniques (p.50-53).

西須久子
刺繍家。JACA日本アートクラフト協会理事。
著書に『はじめてのドロンワーク』(文化出版局)他。
p.6, p.8-9, p.18, p.19, p.22(マフラー), p.23, p.30, p.31, p.32,
p33, p.35, p.38, p.39, p.41, p.43, p.47, p.48の作品を刺繍。
ステッチ・テクニック(p.50-53)を監修。

Yasuko Ito
Embroiderer. Director of Japan Art Craft Association.
p.10, p.11, p.15, p.22(border), p.26-27, p.40, p.42.
Techniques (p.50-53).

伊東保子
刺繍家。JACA日本アートクラフト協会理事。
p.10, p.11, p.15, p.22(ボーダー), p.26-27, p.40, p.42の作品を刺繍。
ステッチ・テクニック (p.50-53)を監修。

Misako Okumura
Embroiderer. Director of Japan Art Craft Association.
p.16, p.21, p.44-45, p.46.

奥村美紗子
刺繍家。JACA日本アートクラフト協会理事。
p.16, p.21, p.44-45, p.46の作品を刺繍。

Mariko Yoshikawa
Embroiderer.
p.12, p.13, p.17, p.20, p.34, p.36, p.37.

吉川真理子
刺繍家。
p.12, p.13, p17, p20, p.34, p36, p37 の作品を刺繍。

Writers of Text

Makiko Komiya
Former curator of Bunka Gakuen Costume Museum.

小宮真喜子
文化学園服飾博物館 元学芸員。

Yoko Yoshimura
Yoko Yoshimura is an expert on the lives and cultures of Japan and France.
"LE VRAI LUXE ENSEIGNE PAR LES FRANÇAIS QUI NE DEPENSENT PAS"
(SHUFUNOTOMOSHA).

吉村葉子
日仏生活文化研究家。
著作に『徹底してお金を使わないフランス人から学んだ本当の贅沢』
(主婦の友社)他。

	ART DIRECTION & BOOK DESIGN	
縄田智子 L'espace	Tomoko Nawata L'espace	

PHOTOGRAPH
長嶺輝明 Teruaki Nagamine

ENGLISH TRANSLATION
杉本まゆみ Mayumi Sugimoto

PATTERN TRACING
株式会社 アズワン Az1 Inc

COLLABORATION
山城美穂子 Mihoko Yamashiro

EDITING
武内千衣子 Chieko Takeuchi

本書は、雄鶏社が2005年に出版した『クロスステッチ フォークロア』を元に貴重な収録作品を追加し、新版化したものです。

材料協力
ディー・エム・シー株式会社
〒101-0035 東京都千代田区神田紺屋町13番地 山東ビル7F
TEL 03-5296-7831　FAX 03-5296-7833
http://www.dmc.com

DMC ANTIQUE COLLECTION

東欧刺繍のモチーフ＆パターン
クロスステッチ フォークロア
CROSS-STITCH FOLKLORE

2018年3月17日　発　行　　　　　NDC594

編　者　誠文堂新光社
発行者　小川雄一
発行所　株式会社 誠文堂新光社
　　　　〒113-0033 東京都文京区本郷3-3-11
　　　　（編集）TEL 03-5805-7285
　　　　（販売）TEL 03-5800-5780
　　　　http://www.seibundo-shinkosha.net/
印刷所　株式会社 大熊整美堂
製本所　株式会社 ブロケード

©2018, La Main Plus.
Patterns of Embroidery Copyright© DOLLFUS MIEG & Cie
Printed in Japan

検印省略
禁・無断転載

落丁・乱丁本はお取り替え致します。

本書のコピー、スキャン、デジタル化等の無断複製は、著作権法上での例外を除き、禁じられています。本書を代行業者等の第三者に依頼してスキャンやデジタル化することは、たとえ個人や家庭内での利用であっても著作権法上認められません。

JCOPY 〈(社)出版者著作権管理機構 委託出版物〉
本書を無断で複製複写（コピー）することは、著作権法上での例外を除き、禁じられています。本書をコピーされる場合は、そのつど事前に、(社)出版者著作権管理機構（TEL 03-3513-6969／FAX 03-3513-6979／e-mail:info@jcopy.or.jp）の許諾を得てください。

ISBN978-4-416-51809-0